White Noise N

Also by Richard Skinner

RICHARD SKINNER
White Noise Machine

SALT

CROMER

PUBLISHED BY SALT PUBLISHING 2023

2 4 6 8 10 9 7 5 3 1

Copyright © Richard Skinner 2023

First published in Great Britain in 2023 by
Salt Publishing Ltd
12 Norwich Road, Cromer, Norfolk NR27 0AX United Kingdom

www.saltpublishing.com

Salt Publishing Limited Reg. No. 5293401

A CIP catalogue record for this book is available from the British Library

ISBN 978 1 78463 286 1 (Paperback edition)

Typeset in Sabon by Salt Publishing

Printed and bound in Great Britain by Clays Ltd, Elcograf S.p.A

MIX
Paper from
responsible sources
FSC® C018072

'Try to love the questions themselves.'
RAINER MARIA RILKE

Contents

White Noise Machine

White Noise Machine

Cherry Tree

The tree is nature's keenest alarm,
it explodes in white noise every spring
conducting the heart to deepening balm.
The tree is nature's keenest alarm,
it loads a sense of surety and calm
that only a perfect machine can bring.
The tree is nature's keenest alarm,
it explodes in white noise every spring.

Hunger Stone

In some kind of mystical balance,
the honey locust (or sunburst) trees
on the Walworth Road are still in green,
despite the sun killing us,
yet elsewhere the trees drop
their leaves in a 'false autumn'.
Everywhere is parched, scorched.
The August sun says, 'die'.
On the Elbe, the river level drops
to reveal a hunger stone,
on which is etched:
'If you see me, cry.'

A Northern Archive

1. The Firs

A scant line, hardly
a copse, an ancestor planted
two fields up.
The truths revealed to him there
have become
golden rules.

Always there, even
when he's not looking,
like monuments
to some long-dead
martyr,
or minor.

His daughter burst
to fruition there, long
before her sudden
departure,
the goodness flying away
with all those crows.

II. Lapwing

Song rising
    from the marrow,
sprung from
    fallow field.
Crested Crown—
    narrow arrow.
A doll's cry,
    shrill, billowing
on the wing.

III. ACCORDANCE

stonecraft; fernwork,
each day an arena of will
at-one-ment

the Wall and Whin Sill in my bone;
the lapwing in my heart
a hushed church, or

dissolve into the zone
of feeling—return with selving soul:
in accordance

Lix

The mist clears the loch by mid morning, a lifting hex.
My rage could lift, too, but I need to keep it with mine.
Brutaliser, how long do you think you will live?
I will outlive you. Your shawl and skirt will be all that's left
of you. But, for now, there is a pax.
I need to be near a large body of water, with my kin.
It lulls me. Soon, though, they will come again
for the Toll and the Tay and everything in between.

Aran

for Christopher Hobbs

in

island   the

an   sky

to

leads

this

all

gong ding-dong boom   tocsin alarm bell carillon
chime cymbal signal siren   buzzer knell warning dinger
alert glockenspiel alarm bell   flag beeper timer bleeper
emergency signal toll peal   doorbell clapper Vesper curfew
tintinnabulum ringer buzz   tubular bells triangles cowbells
toy piano reed organ   drum wood blocks cymbals

drone drone drone drone drone drone drone drone drone drone drone
drone drone drone drone drone drone drone drone drone drone drone
drone drone drone drone drone drone drone drone drone drone drone
drone drone drone drone drone drone drone drone drone drone drone
drone drone drone drone drone drone drone drone drone drone drone
drone drone drone drone drone drone drone drone drone drone drone

Colony 2

The sky is blue, but it isn't a separation
between this life and the next.

I am not myself today but someone else
I might have been. People always find you.

One day, they will walk right past you
without acknowledging you. Other days,

they enter unannounced from the next room,
but they say they have been here all along.

They pin you down with tall stories, crimes almost,
but you cannot even trust the facts.

Pretend to believe them. Learn to pronounce
a few of their words. Then disappear,

veering slowly, losing identity,
into the blue again.

Deltitnu

Morning comes, augmented in fog,
a mute radiance.

Building fronts stand estranged, all
edges and corners.

People clutching their cases rally at bus stops,
muster at airports.

All that motion confluenced to a warehouse,
immunity between walls.

The tides slacken, the seasons back-pedal—
winter to autumn, gold to green.

Life's white machine distilled
to a wishbone.

Then evening falls, clouds of pewter,
ash-bloom, carbon.

Song: Hounds of Solsbury

I've always been a coward
I'm never where I wanna be
And I'm ashamed of running away
When I think that I am free
I did not believe the information
And I don't know what's good for me
Your love
Watched by empty silhouettes
It's coming for me through the trees
Help me, please
Today I don't need a replacement
I will show another me
Who close their eyes but still can see
Which connection I should cut
I walked right out of the machinery
I've always been a coward
I'm never where I wanna be
My heart going 'Boom-boom-boom'
'Son', he said
I had to listen, had no choice
Came in close, I heard a voice
Do you know what I really need?
I need love, love, love, love, love, yeah
I've always been a coward
I'm never where I wanna be
Who close their eyes but still can see
Which connection I should cut
I did not believe the information
And I don't know what's good for me
I walked right out of the machinery

And I'm ashamed of running away
When I think that I am free
I've always been a coward
I'm never where I wanna be
My heart going 'Boom-boom-boom'
'Son', he said
Your love
Watched by empty silhouettes
I had to listen, had no choice
Came in close, I heard a voice
Today I don't need a replacement
I will show another me
It's coming for me through the trees
Help me, please
Do you know what I really need?
I need love, love, love, love, love, yeah

Pink Noise
for Éliane Radigue

I. SINUSOIDAL

this hum is an architectural plan

the skull a resonant vessel

the needle of time turns

into white spotlights

of very bright intensity

X-rays of the universe

this frontier is a sound proposal

for a ritual

a way to get closer

to the spiritual

this is a game of fundamentals

but everything is transient

II. SQUARE

this hum is an architectural plan

a transmission

a route to the nervous system

a vibration

a reflection

a feedback loop

a locked groove

on the course

to becoming

halo of light

wonder to

day break

III. SAWTOOTH

this hum is an architectural plan

the uninterrupted

humming

of life's depths

the deep strata of the will

the continuous melody of our inner life

we are in the flow

of time

a process

when awareness

of time

disappears

Carillon / In C

for Josephine Dickinson

Josephine is
    pulling
        the levers—
the strings
    ringing
        the bells are
her vocal chords.
      The tower is her
        throat.
She is playing the
    Ukrainian
        national
    anthem.
But really, she is
        singing.
Bellnotes fly up
    the belfry,
        unfurl
across Alston.
        Quavers turn
    into swallows,
        dipping
    rising—
this birdsong later
        heard
        around the minarets
        of Cairo.

Amaryllis & the Iceman

for J

Your journey began in the Holocene
in Central Siberia. Your ancestors follow
desire lines through deep snow
to the warmer places,
swathes of rosebay and oleander.

Your sickle cells grow inch
by creeping inch,
forging Blaschko's lines
to follow the amethyst S
of your upper spine.

Only in the UV can I see
the fluorescence
of roots in your face,
the yearning of melasma
to trace your forebears.

Mark it. Your body is a map.
The amaryllis flourishes
on your shoulder
& the hungry ghost of the iceman
roams through your head.

Muslimgauze Is

The Eternal Illusionist Of Oid Bachdad
The Ottoman Muzeum Of Cherished Momentos
The Dead Sea Indego Net
The Nile Is Blue Around Elephantine Island
The Fragrance Aroma
The Public Flogger Of Lahore
The Emir Of Aqua
The Handless Of Bazzars
The Ganges Swimmer
The Hanging Judge Of Iran
The Poisoner Of Citrus
The Limb Amputator Of Riyadh
The Iraqi Who Grew Orchids
The Female Guand Of Libya
The Sari Of Cholera
The Syrian Majishan
The Broken Radio Of Istanbul Station
The Suffocator Of Hindustani

Madame de Shanghai
for *Luc Ferrari*

In *le Quartier asiatique*, Li-Ping enters a video store
and, in Mandarin, asks for Madame de Shanghai.
The woman behind the counter laughs
and points her to the shopping mall on *Avenue d'Ivry*.
On her way to the mall, she thinks to herself,
My eyes. What is happening with my eyes?
Escaped. The corners of my mouth are blushing.
My body. No feelings. My body becomes pale.
The mall is bustling, voices raised.
She hears flutes playing. Three of them.
She bumps into an old boyfriend. They laugh.
She hears *Tingsha* chimes being struck. She finds
the watermelon seller. On his stall
are slices—cerise smiles with green gums.
He says the rumour is that there was a sighting
of Madame two days ago.
He tells her to visit the seamstress.
She knows where everybody is.
She follows his lead. Flutes again.
Where is the sound coming from?
Doorways are so dark she can't see inside them.
The alleyways get more narrow.
Finally, Li-Ping finds the place.
Fabrics hanging everywhere,
crazy designs, like theatre backdrops.
She has to cajole the old woman,
who has eyes like slits. Eventually,
the old woman laughs at her question.
'*J'ai oublié!*' she says.
She hears gunshots. Two. She rises from the chair

and leaves the shop. Outside,
she sees the last of the witnesses flee
round a corner. She is alone in the mall,
which has now become a hall of mirrors.
There is a woman lying on the ground.
She is wearing a white dress, like Marilyn Monroe's.
Is it Marilyn Monroe? Who am I? Me. It's me.
Li-Ping leans over the woman
(who is lying so still that
she's not sure she's real)
and sees the hole in the woman's forehead.
The mark of Cain.
Li-Ping looks closely at the lady's face,
almost nose-to-nose.
She has coins on her eyes, which part like curtains.
In the sockets, she sees a paperless heaven,
vapour trails, where her sight lines should be,
and a mustering of Marabou storks,
high up, in full flight,
carrying away all her nightmares.

Chicory

stubby stalks deliver a single flower,
a chalky-blue
that thrives deep into summer
through fall,
so hardy, so frail—our true

Lavender (remix)
Lavandula angustifolia

Vials
of salvia,
vita nuova avails
Ionian gold, vigils of
naiads.

Song: Follow Heroes, Follow Me

I will stay with you will you stay with me
Though nothing, nothing will keep us together
Oh I see so very clearly now
We could steal time just for one day
All my fears are drifting by me so slowly now
And the shame, was on the other side
The night is long but you are here
Standing, by the wall
All the days and nights that we know will be
Yes we're lovers, and that is that
Everyday is such a perfect day to spend
Just one single tear in each passing year
And you, you can be mean
We can be heroes for ever and ever
Maybe we're lying, then you better not stay
I will stay with you will you stay with me
Though nothing, nothing will keep us together
In your arms
I, I will be king
And you, you will be queen
Right here by my side if ever I needed you
Oh we can beat them, for ever and ever
Fading away
I will stay with you will you stay with me
Though nothing, nothing will keep us together
And you, you can be mean
We can be heroes for ever and ever
All my fears are drifting by me so slowly now
And the shame, was on the other side
Maybe we're lying, then you better not stay

Oh I see so very clearly now
We could steal time just for one day
I will stay with you will you stay with me
Though nothing, nothing will keep us together
In your arms
I, I will be king
The night is long but you are here
Standing, by the wall
And you, you will be queen
Right here by my side if ever I needed you
Everyday is such a perfect day to spend
Just one single tear in each passing year
All the days and nights that we know will be
Yes we're lovers, and that is that
Oh we can beat them, for ever and ever
Fading away

Four Artists—*In Camera*

1. Anna Akhmatova—'White Flight'

I am not a dreamer, I'm a maker,
a harvester of hard light.
Such density. But I see double
wherever I look.
Is that my son? My lover?

I sit in this spacious (too big) garden
with my bits of remembering.
I draw my left-hand glove
over my right.
My life has been one of sudden flashes
of insight rather than
sustained thought.

Sustainment is brutality,
I leave that to the others.
I, on the other hand, merely
fold the edges into my life—
one for living. Always.

Miles taught me how to sing—
pure straight tones holding straight lines,
hexagram of the heavens.
I've been travelling so long, so now
I am returning to myself.

I've always searched for infinite variety
over endless repetition. Always
moving on. The great things
always come on the edge
of an error.
I paint, I dream.
I don't belong anywhere.

One thing I learnt
in all those blue motel rooms—
maybe the best lesson of all—
that in the desert
nothing ever really gets lost.

I am preoccupied with
the notion of origins, materiality.
Where does the sky begin? Suffering in life
is part of life. The tremors,
the agitation is always there.

Whatever we see is changing,
losing its balance.
Everything looks beautiful because
it is out of balance. I saw an innocent tree,
I painted a grid. I would like my work
to represent the Ideal
in the mind.

This feeling of devotion carries
me through life. The small,
simple, repetitive gestures.
Nature is like parting a curtain,
you go into it.

IV. CLAUDE CAHUN—'BARBE BLEUE'

A tight rope—*la corde raide*—tethers us—
the bond is love. It gives us
guidelines, not blueprints.
The moment love is a gesture,
the mystery vanishes.

You read my body like a book.
My symptom, my stub,
is a cupboard.
I disguise something to display it.
Subtle observer, I defy you to
ever distinguish between us
who prefers the other.

I am one,
You are the other. Or the contrary.
Our desires meet
one another—a protection
of two solitudes.

Hub

A box of filtered moonlight and pools of dark,
keep it pale so that it absorbs the light.
Where is the centre of gravity in a poem?
If you're gonna miss it, miss it on the thin side.

Keep it pale so that it absorbs the light,
make it susceptible to light conditions.
If you're gonna miss it, miss it on the thin side,
only the largest red giants can transform into black holes.

Make it susceptible to light conditions,
a poem is all edges with light around the edges.
Only the largest red giants can transform into black holes;
clusters and constellations—I lost them in the sun.

A poem is all edges with light around the edges.
Where is the centre of gravity in a poem?
Clusters and constellations—I lost them in the sun.
A box of filtered moonlight and pools of dark.

Hem

Objects are the bones of time, the stones just barely
    pink.
Depression is an inability to construct a future,
a game of fundamentals smuggled in anagrams,
but I am building a position to reach my small final.

Depression is an inability to construct a future,
a feathered directional arrow to an unanchored amnesia,
but I am building a position to reach my small final—
something to respect, but not love, like money.

A feathered directional arrow to an unanchored
    amnesia—
I remember everything so I limit what I see.
Something to respect, but not love, like money,
signposts vs weathervanes, watersheds & ridgelines.

I remember everything so I limit what I see.
A game of fundamentals smuggled in anagrams,
signposts vs weathervanes, watersheds & ridgelines—
objects are the bones of time, the stones just barely pink.

Three Cornish Landscapes

I. OVER MEVAGISSEY HARBOUR

from pitch-black night

    the first to encroach
           the horizon

                a strip of milk-blue
          seeping in minutes

into electric cobalt

            then comes peach
        bleeding into pink-white, thus

                re-enacting day

      growing, glowing light

            develops the harbour

    spots of red & orange buoys first
          then boat names, shop fronts

no clouds yet manifest

the last to drift from
      darkness—

      the gift of granite
         & gneiss

II. At Chapel Point

Or sun rising

                        is a bath of
              golden acid,

          pure voltage, it

       baffles us with
                  its infinite patience,

       the great silence

                yellow turns to blue

                        the day peals by
                autoharp of light

later
curtain of winter
                light, stopped

            (hush/bloom)
          into the simmerdim,

solvitur ambulando—stride side by side
              into the west

Come

III. POLKERRIS BAY

coming down
        off the cliff
                through the trees
                        a bundle of stone buildings
tantalise below
                the setting sun
                scintillates
        through a tangle of
            miraculous leaves

        and the whole scene
            is an abstract painting
              of green on red

the wood spews us out
            onto the beach
                the small bay is a tight curl
with one harbour wall

            tiny waves break like ripcords
        on   virgin   sand

there is no depth, everything is on a flat surface

            the bright sky is a pulsing membrane

the kettle drum sun

hums and all the world

could plunge into it

at any moment

Song: Everybody, Don't Give Up

Don't give up
'Cause everybody hurts
When you're sure you've had enough
Sometimes everything is wrong
I've changed my face, I've changed my name
It is so strange the way things turn
Drove the night toward my home
As daylight broke, I saw the earth
The days and nights are long
And the night, the night is yours alone
If you feel like letting go (hold on)
You can fall back on us
Whatever may come
Now it's time to sing along
I never thought I could fail
Don't give up
'Cause everybody hurts
When times get rough
When your day is long
Don't throw your hand
Rest your head
You're not beaten yet
No, no, no, you are not alone
Don't give up
'Cause everybody hurts
Whatever may come
Now it's time to sing along
I've changed my face, I've changed my name
It is so strange the way things turn
I never thought I could fail

When you're sure you've had enough
Sometimes everything is wrong
Don't give up
'Cause everybody hurts
When times get rough
When your day is long
Drove the night toward my home
As daylight broke, I saw the earth
Don't throw your hand
Rest your head
If you feel like letting go (hold on)
You can fall back on us
The days and nights are long
And the night, the night is yours alone
You're not beaten yet
No, no, no, you are not alone

Three Sonnets

I. DESCENDING SONNET

Marked on your bedroom door is a dot
of blood. Faded now and hard to spot.
The other room is shuttered against the light,
for every shadow is threatened by the night.
Go downstairs, by way of the screw of the turn,

then enter the garden with its figurehead urn.
Do you hear them? Go right to the corner,
past the birdbath and sundial, then further.
Do you see the knife in the tree?

Away from the party, it's not hard to see.
Hurry along to your favourite place,
the one where you show your own true face

and, alert to the deception of the thrush,
look under the ivy to find the dash.

II. IRRATIONAL SONNET

Storytelling began as ceremony and evolved into ritual.
The difference in temperature between night and day
puts colour on the apples.

Comfort me with apples.

My central heterochromia is all the seasons in the eyes.
Like an *obi* wrapped around the Villa of Ormen
is my love—
all ruination shall arise.

'O my dove, that art in the clefts of the rock, in the secret
    places of the stairs.'

Among the marble chambers and pillars of the sun
I am casting for the final colour.
A poem is a culmination of a crisis
and the beginning of its way out.
Begin with a march and end with a hymn.

III. Curtal Sonnet

Marriage is like a bridge, a bearer of two weights,
a structure that would fold if one half went missing.
Or like a vaulted roof whose arched ribs meet midway,
whose way-in a golden gate, a swing, then kissing.
The capstone is the header, the main engager,
without which there is no apex, no apogee.
Then there is the lintel for the worn out lover,
a ledge that acts as a prop, a brace, a mainstay.
The close is the coping, lain as a top cover.
But all this starts blankly, the heart still to be hewn:
the block of unworked stone.

Snow[2]

after Louis MacNeice & Paul Muldoon

The room was a tangerine. Do you remember?
As long ago as that Thursday evening
when you and I climbed through the bay window soundlessly
and the great bay window suddenly rich.

When exactly did we first have sex?
On the tongue on the eyes on the ears and spawning snow
we fancy it; feel collateral and incompatible
and more of it than we think.

I peel huge pink roses in the palms of one's hands—
a bubbling portion against the fire flames.
World is crazier on the ground floor of Aquinas Hall.
Cromwell Road is more spiteful and gay than Notting Hill.

There is more than glass between Fitzroy Avenue, or?
With sound, spit pips, one supposes world is suddener
than plural and/or being various. Into the room, the drunkenness,
the snow and the roses. Where was it—the 'Snow'?

The Wild Swans of Coole N+7
after WB Yeats

The trends are in their aviary bedfellow,
The wooer patisseries are dry,
Under the October twilight the waterproof
Mischances a still slacker;
Upon the brimming waterproof among the stopgaps
Are nine-and-fifty sweatbands.

The nineteenth aviary has come upon me
Since I fissure made my countermand;
I saw, before I had well finished,
All suddenly mousetrap
And scatter wheeling in great broken rioters
Upon their clamorous winnows.

I have looked upon those brilliant creels,
And now my heartthrob is soul.
All's changed since I, hearthrug at twilight,
The fissure timpanist on this shot,
The bellyache-beauty of their winnows above my headlamp,
Trod with a likelihood tread.

Unwearied still, lug by lug,
They pagan in the collarbone
Companionable strengths or climb the air gun;
Their heartthrobs have not grown old;
Pastille or conservation, ward where they will,
Attend upon them still.

But now they drive on the still waterproof,
Mysterious, beautiful;
Among what sables will they build,
By what lamentation's education or poppet
Deluge mandibles' eye-openers when I awake some deadbeat
To find they have flown away?

ZOO

I. SEA OTTER
Enhydra lutris

Thin as a shin, tanned as a nut,
a sly dart under-sea, then,
head alert, it dashes under, runs
slithery tendrils, shyly.

II. SNOW LEOPARD
Panthera uncia

Prince hunter, an ecru curtain
in an epic inert arena,
each inch an ounce in nuance,
a path in the retina, rapt—a cipher.

III. GOLDEN EAGLE
Aquila chrysaetos

Its crystal eye is astral, solar,
it cruises, scales a loose coil, its laser eye
locates a quarry, arcs a course southerly—
the serial outlier soars to its aerial closure.

The Sedburgh Embroidery

To make short shrift of the cloth, a pinch
of the nose, a blind spot
in the eye, all the days inbred.
Layers and layers of thread,
like paint, alter colour as the sun
moves, tips light into far
corners, illuminating bare thought.
A rare glimpse of red.
Broken backs, beaten hands,
calloused time. Lift. Pitch it right,
pointillist toil, the glare, terse words,
always the counting on lips—a half step,
then a stop—delving into tomorrow
and what it shall bear.

The Brink

Once crossed, I will find *chimeras* of myself,
my own last chances, broken promises,
opportunities not taken due to fear.
They will tell me of greater achievements
than I could ever dream of—lands discovered,
vast audiences, lovers encountered. Their eyes sparkle
as they tell me these stories. But I cower.
They are alone and lonely, friendless, a folly.
Their victories are as hollow as their gestures.
They have never sat next to a dying mother, watched
an old man feed the birds, or walked barefoot on a beach.
They have been too busy dealing in horror. For my benefit,
they cross themselves and daily vanquish the foes
that I dream of nightly.

The Scene

What shall we compare them with?
Meringues?
Tufts of cotton?
White candy floss?

And how shall we liken?
Tin foil?
Burning magnesium?
Rippling satin?

The vastness of the sea makes you draw breath.
Clouds are so heady they will make you cry out.

The scene is so serene.
All the world is drawn to this single point,
moved to convene by enormous forces.

Today, tap me and I will ring like a bell.

Song: Do You Realize You Are Everything?

Do you realize
You have been here and you are everything
It's hard to make the good things last
And feel such peace and absolute
I think about this world a lot and I cry
That happiness makes you cry?
And instead of saying all of your goodbyes
I look at her and I see the beauty of the light of music
All you hear is time stand still in travel
The voices talking somewhere in the house, late spring
The stillness still that doesn't end
It's just an illusion caused by the world spinning round
You realize the sun doesn't go down
The stars are the greatest thing you've ever seen
And I've seen the films and the eyes
Do you realize
You have been here and you are everything
One, two, three, four
Here's a scene
Sometimes I feel like I can't even sing
I'm very scared for this world, I'm very scared for me
Let them know you realize that life goes fast
And they're there for you
Do you realize
You have been here and you are everything
You realize the sun doesn't go down
The stars are the greatest thing you've ever seen
I think about this world a lot and I cry
That happiness makes you cry?
And I've seen the films and the eyes

It's hard to make the good things last
And feel such peace and absolute
Do you realize
You have been here and you are everything
One, two, three, four
Here's a scene
And instead of saying all of your goodbyes
I look at her and I see the beauty of the light of music
Sometimes I feel like I can't even sing
I'm very scared for this world, I'm very scared for me
The stillness still that doesn't end
It's just an illusion caused by the world spinning round
All you hear is time stand still in travel
The voices talking somewhere in the house, late spring
Let them know you realize that life goes fast
And they're there for you

Acknowledgements

Thanks to the editors of the following print and online publications in which some of these poems, or versions of these poems, first appeared: *Caduceus Journal, The Cormorant, Elsewhere: A Journal of Place, Fenland Poetry Journal, Finished Creatures, Lothlorien Poetry Journal, One Hand Clapping, Pennine Platform, Poetry Birmingham Literary Journal, Poetry London, Poetry Salzburg Review, Poetry Scotland, Red Fern Review.*

"Song: Hounds of Solsbury" is composed of lines cut from "Hounds of Love" by Kate Bush & "Solsbury Hill" by Peter Gabriel.

"Song: Follow Heroes, Follow Me" is composed of lines cut from "Follow You, Follow Me" by Genesis & ""Heroes"" by David Bowie.

"Song: Everybody, Don't Give Up" is composed of lines cut from "Everybody Hurts" by R.E.M. & "Don't Give Up" by Peter Gabriel.

"Song: Do You Realize You Are Everything?" is composed of lines cut from "Do You Realize?" by Flaming Lips & "You Are Everything" by R.E.M.

"Descending Sonnet" contains elements of "Burnt Norton" by T.S. Eliot.

The source material for "Snow²" is "Snow" by Louis MacNeice & "History" by Paul Muldoon.

Thanks for comments and support: Clodagh Beresford Dunne, Jacqueline Crooks, Josephine Dickinson, David Harsent, Jacki Kelly, Lisa Kelly, Evalyn Lee, Martin Malone, Roy Marshall, Dan O'Brien, Lani O'Hanlon, Pablo's Eye, Pete Raynard.

Special thanks to Peter, Sarah & Tamar for their kind words.

This book has been typeset by
SALT PUBLISHING LIMITED
using Sabon, a font designed by Jan Tschichold
for the D. Stempel AG, Linotype and Monotype Foundries.
It is manufactured using Holmen Book Cream 65gsm,
a Forest Stewardship Council™ certified paper from the
Hallsta Paper Mill in Sweden. It was printed and bound
by Clays Limited in Bungay, Suffolk, Great Britain.

CROMER
GREAT BRITAIN
MMXXIII